D0312179

5430000507940 4

IT'S Raining Fish!: COOL FACTS ABOUT THE WEATHER

by Kaitlyn Duling

raintree

a Capstone company — publishers for children

Raintree is an imprint of Capstone Global Library Limited, a company incorporated in England and Wales having its registered office at 264 Banbury Road, Oxford, OX2 7DY – Registered company number: 6695582

www.raintree.co.uk
myorders@raintree.co.uk

Edited by Meg Gaertner
Designed by Becky Daum
Production by Colleen McLaren
Printed and bound in India

ISBN 978 1 4747 7460 4 (hardback)
ISBN 978 1 4747 8245 6 (paperback)

British Library Cataloguing in Publication Data
A full catalogue record for this book is available from the British Library.

Acknowledgements
We would like to thank the following for permission to reproduce photographs: iStockphoto: diatrezor, 22–23, hadynyah, 12–13, Ji Feliciano, 7, 28, petesphotography, 26–27, Placebo365, 21, Wavebreakmedia, 30–31; Shutterstock Images: Caleb Holder, 14–15, fibPhoto, 8–9, Jeff Gammons StormVisuals, 5, John D. Sirlin, 18–19, MDay Photography, 17, PrabhatK, 25, Romolo Tavani, cover (bottom), Tony Campbell, cover (top), Yurio1978, 11
Every effort has been made to contact copyright holders of material reproduced in this book. Any omissions will be rectified in subsequent printings if notice is given to the publisher.

We would like to thank Dr Elinor Martin, Assistant Professor of Meteorology, for her help with this book.

CONTENTS

WILD Weather

Some storms are made of dust. Lightning burns hotter than the Sun. Clouds can drop frogs along with water. **Weather** is always changing. It is powerful. It is wild. Extreme weather can be amazing!

One hundred lightning bolts hit the Earth every second.

BURNING UP AND
Cooling Off

The Earth's hottest day happened in California, USA. It was 10 July 1913. The place was **Furnace** Creek. The temperature reached 56.7 degrees Celsius (134 degrees Fahrenheit)!

DEATH VALLEY

Furnace Creek is in Death Valley, USA. This is in the Mojave Desert. Death Valley is one of the Earth's hottest places.

Despite its heat, Death Valley is a national park and visitors go there every year.

7

The city of Verkhoyansk, Siberia, experiences the greatest temperature range in the world.

ICY DESERT

Antarctica may be cold. But it is still a desert. It does not get much rain or snow.

BRRRR!

Earth's coldest place is in Antarctica. Record lows happen in a mountain range there. The lowest temperature was taken by **satellite**. It was -93 degrees Celsius (-136 degrees Fahrenheit). People do not live there. But people do live in very cold places. Towns in Siberia get harsh winters. Temperatures can drop to -68 degrees Celsius (-90 degrees Fahrenheit).

CHAPTER 3

CLOUDS
and Wind

Clouds can come in crazy shapes. Some clouds look like layers of discs. They sometimes look like **UFOs**. Other clouds look like they have been hole-punched. A brief snowstorm can affect part of the cloud. It leaves behind a hole in the cloud.

Lenticular clouds can look like UFOs.

MOUNT EVEREST

Mount Everest is the world's tallest mountain. Jet streams hit its peak. People who climb to the top feel the jet stream.

WIND POWER

The strongest winds happen miles above the Earth's surface. **Jet streams** are very fast winds. They can move at 440 kilometres (275 miles) per hour. Aeroplane pilots try not to fly against these winds. They fly above the jet stream. Or they fly in the same direction as the wind.

Climbers of Mount Everest face very cold winds.

Dust storms occur mostly in dry areas.

Wind can whip up sand, dirt or dust. It can turn into a storm. These storms are called "black **blizzards**". They can happen all around the world.

DUST STORMS

Dust storms happen on other planets too. Scientists have seen dust storms on Mars.

CHAPTER 4

STORMS on the Horizon

A **hurricane** is a type of **tropical** storm. Its winds can flatten houses. Hurricane Irma struck in 2017. Its winds covered an area larger than England. They moved at 298 kilometres (185 miles) per hour.

Hurricanes can produce **tornadoes**. Hurricane Ivan hit the United States in 2004. It created 127 tornadoes. Tornado outbreaks can be dangerous. One happened in 2011. Over three days, 349 tornadoes struck 21 US states.

Hurricanes can cause massive amounts of flooding.

ZAP!

Lightning bolts strike during storms. They are bright and hot. In fact, they are five times hotter than the Sun! They can reach 27,700 degrees Celsius (50,000 degrees Fahrenheit).

Lightning starts in the clouds. Most of it stays there. But some bolts strike the ground. They zap at 300,000,000 kilometres (200,000,000 miles) per hour!

Thunder is the sound made by lightning.

CHAPTER 5

FALLING FROM the Sky

Rain and snow often fall from the sky. But strange things have also "rained" down onto the Earth. They include frogs, fish, snakes and meat. The cause can be a waterspout. This is similar to a tornado. But it forms over water. It lifts things in its path. Then it drops them like rain elsewhere.

WATER WATCH

Waterspouts are spinning columns of water. The water does not come from the sea. It comes from the clouds.

Many waterspouts form in the Florida Keys, USA.

Most hail falls as tiny balls of ice.

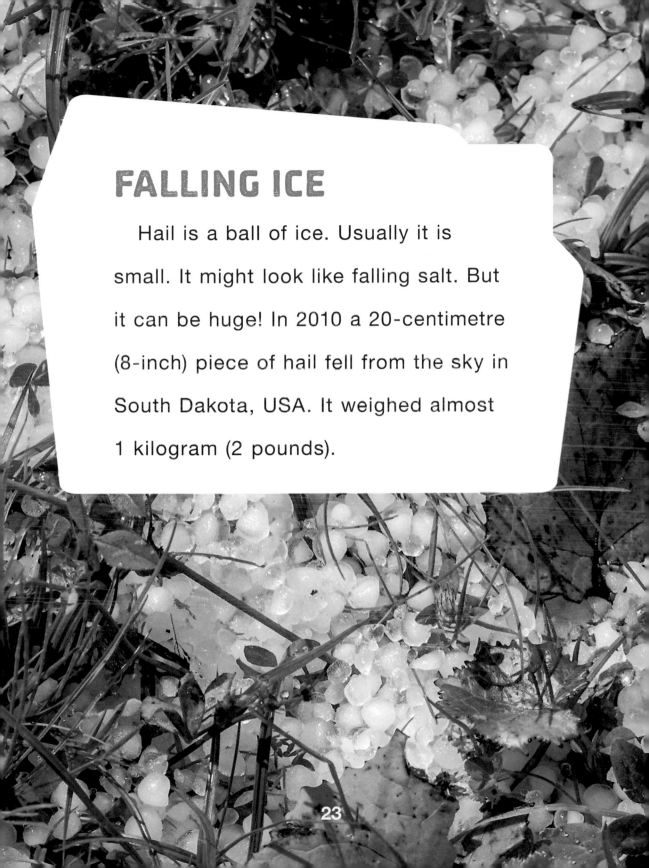

FALLING ICE

Hail is a ball of ice. Usually it is small. It might look like falling salt. But it can be huge! In 2010 a 20-centimetre (8-inch) piece of hail fell from the sky in South Dakota, USA. It weighed almost 1 kilogram (2 pounds).

SNOW MOTION

Some people make snowballs in the winter. But sometimes snowballs make themselves. Wind blows across a snowy field. It pushes the snow along a path. The snow forms a ball and rolls. It leaves a trail behind itself. These giant snowballs are called snow rollers.

Snow rollers are also known as snow doughnuts.

Snow can roll itself. Fish can fall from the sky. Hurricanes can be larger than countries. Weather is all around us. It can be amazing!

Supercell thunderstorms can bring large hail, strong winds and tornadoes.

GLOSSARY

blizzard
a harsh snowstorm with strong winds

furnace
a structure used to heat things to high temperatures

hurricane
a large tropical storm that includes circular winds

jet stream
a fast-moving river of air high in the sky

satellite
a man-made object that moves around the Earth

tornado
a strong column of wind that spins quickly

tropical
having to do with the tropics, the region of the Earth near the equator

weather
conditions that include heat, cold, storms, clouds, pressure, wind, moisture and more

UFO
an unidentified flying object, sometimes claimed to be an alien spaceship

1. During hot summers in the northern hemisphere, It mIght feel lIke the Earth Is close to the Sun. But it is the opposite. Earth is closest to the Sun during winter. Earth is furthest from the Sun during summer. The distance to the Sun does not create Earth's seasons. Earth's tilt on its axis does. The tilt affects the angle at which the Sun's light hits Earth.

2. Some thunderstorms actually produce snow instead of rain. This is called "thundersnow".

3. Chinook winds blow east from the Rocky Mountains in the US. They bring warm air during winter months. They are sometimes called "snow eaters". They get rid of snow quickly. They are named after the Chinook Native Americans.

ACTIVITY

WEATHER TRACKER

Scientists study the weather. They take careful notes and measurements. You can study the weather too. Choose a city in another country. You can compare the weather at home and in that city.

Study the weather for one week. Pay close attention to the weather in your neighbourhood. Take the temperature every morning, at noon, and at night. Write down if it rained or snowed. Were there clouds, or was the sky clear? Look up the pressure and humidity too. Write down your findings in a chart. You can include drawings or photos.

At the same time, study the weather in the other city. Look up the weather information online. Make a chart for that place too. When the week is over, look at your two charts. How was the weather in the two cities the same? How was it different?

FIND OUT MORE

Interested in wacky weather? Check out these resources.

Books

50 Things You Should Know About: Wild Weather, Anna Claybourne (QED, 2016)

Totally Amazing Facts About Weather, Jaclyn Jaycox (Raintree, 2018)

Websites

DK Find Out!: Weather
www.dkfindout.com/uk/earth/weather

Met Office: Weather for kids
www.metoffice.gov.uk/learning/weather-for-kids

INDEX